D1008052

To:

_____

From:

_____

Poems
on
Nature

Poems

on

Nature

STERLING
New York

STERLING
New York

An Imprint of Sterling Publishing Co., Inc.

STERLING and the distinctive Sterling logo are registered trademarks
of Sterling Publishing Co., Inc.

Cover illustration and compilation © 2022 Sterling Publishing Co., Inc.

ISBN 978-1-4549-4476-8

Library of Congress Control Number: 2021950961

Distributed in Canada by Sterling Publishing Co., Inc.
c/o Canadian Manda Group, 664 Annette Street
Toronto, Ontario M6S 2C8, Canada
Distributed in the United Kingdom by GMC Distribution Services
Castle Place, 166 High Street, Lewes, East Sussex BN7 1XU, England
Distributed in Australia by NewSouth Books
University of New South Wales, Sydney, NSW 2052, Australia

For information about custom editions, special sales, and premium
and corporate purchases, please contact Sterling Special Sales
at specialsales@sterlingpublishing.com.

Manufactured in the United States

2 4 6 8 10 9 7 5 3

sterlingpublishing.com

Interior design by Rich Hazelton

Contents

Air

Sea

Land

Air

To make a prairie it takes
a clover and one bee

Emily Dickinson

To make a prairie it takes a clover and one bee,—
One clover, and a bee,
And revery.
The revery alone will do,
If bees are few.

To a Butterfly

William Wordsworth

Stay near me—do not take thy flight!
A little longer stay in sight!
Much converse do I find in thee,
Historian of my infancy!
Float near me; do not yet depart!
Dead times revive in thee:
Thou bring'st, gay creature as thou art!
A solemn image to my heart,
My father's family!

Oh! pleasant, pleasant were the days,
The time, when, in our childish plays,
My sister Emmeline and I
Together chased the butterfly!
A very hunter did I rush
Upon the prey:—with leaps and springs
I followed on from brake to bush;
But she, God love her, feared to brush
The dust from off its wings.

Sympathy

Paul Laurence Dunbar

I know what the caged bird feels, alas!
    When the sun is bright on the upland slopes;
When the wind stirs soft through the springing grass,
And the river flows like a stream of glass;
    When the first bird sings and the first bud opes,
And the faint perfume from its chalice steals—
I know what the caged bird feels!

I know why the caged bird beats his wing
    Till its blood is red on the cruel bars;
For he must fly back to his perch and cling
When he fain would be on the bough a-swing;
    And a pain still throbs in the old, old scars
And they pulse again with a keener sting—
I know why he beats his wing!

I know why the caged bird sings, ah me,
    When his wing is bruised and his bosom sore,—
When he beats his bars and he would be free;
It is not a carol of joy or glee,
    But a prayer that he sends from his heart's deep core,
But a plea, that upward to Heaven he flings—
I know why the caged bird sings!

Answer to a Child's Question

Samuel Taylor Coleridge

Do you ask what the birds say? The Sparrow, the Dove,
The Linnet and Thrush say, "I love and I love!"
In the winter they're silent—the wind is so strong;
What it says, I don't know, but it sings a loud song.
But green leaves, and blossoms, and sunny warm weather,
And singing, and loving—all come back together.
But the Lark is so brimful of gladness and love,
The green fields below him, the blue sky above,
That he sings, and he sings; and for ever sings he—
"I love my Love, and my Love loves me!"

Ode to a Nightingale

John Keats

I

My heart aches, and a drowsy numbness pains
    My sense, as though of hemlock I had drunk,
Or emptied some dull opiate to the drains
    One minute past, and Lethe-wards had sunk:
'Tis not through envy of thy happy lot,
    But being too happy in thine happiness,—
        That thou, light-winged Dryad of the trees
        In some melodious plot
    Of beechen green, and shadows numberless,
        Singest of summer in full-throated ease.

II

O, for a draught of vintage! that hath been
    Cool'd a long age in the deep-delved earth,
Tasting of Flora and the country green,
    Dance, and Provençal song, and sunburnt mirth!
O for a beaker full of the warm South,
    Full of the true, the blushful Hippocrene,
        With beaded bubbles winking at the brim,
        And purple-stained mouth;
    That I might drink, and leave the world unseen,
        And with thee fade away into the forest
        dim:

III

Fade far away, dissolve, and quite forget
 What thou among the leaves hast never known,
The weariness, the fever, and the fret
 Here, where men sit and hear each other groan;
Where palsy shakes a few, sad, last gray hairs,
  Where youth grows pale, and spectre-thin, and dies;
   Where but to think is to be full of sorrow
    And leaden-eyed despairs,
  Where Beauty cannot keep her lustrous eyes,
   Or new Love pine at them beyond
    to-morrow.

IV

Away! away! for I will fly to thee,
 Not charioted by Bacchus and his pards,
But on the viewless wings of Poesy,
 Though the dull brain perplexes and retards:
Already with thee! tender is the night,
  And haply the Queen-Moon is on her throne,
   Cluster'd around by all her starry Fays;
    But here there is no light,
  Save what from heaven is with the breezes blown
   Through verdurous glooms and winding
    mossy ways.

V

I cannot see what flowers are at my feet,
 Nor what soft incense hangs upon the boughs,
But, in embalmed darkness, guess each sweet
 Wherewith the seasonable month endows

The grass, the thicket, and the fruit-tree wild;
　　White hawthorn, and the pastoral eglantine;
　　　　Fast fading violets cover'd up in leaves;
　　　　　And mid-May's eldest child,
　　The coming musk-rose, full of dewy wine,
　　　　The murmurous haunt of flies on summer
　　　　　eves.

VI

Darkling I listen; and, for many a time
　　I have been half in love with easeful Death,
Call'd him soft names in many a mused rhyme,
　　To take into the air my quiet breath;
Now more than ever seems it rich to die,
　　To cease upon the midnight with no pain,
　　　　While thou art pouring forth thy soul abroad
　　　　　In such an ecstasy!
　　Still wouldst thou sing, and I have ears in vain—
　　　　To thy high requiem become a sod.

VII

Thou wast not born for death, immortal Bird!
　　No hungry generations tread thee down;
The voice I hear this passing night was heard
　　In ancient days by emperor and clown:
Perhaps the self-same song that found a path
　　Through the sad heart of Ruth, when, sick for home,
　　　　She stood in tears amid the alien corn;
　　　　　The same that oft-times hath
　　Charm'd magic casements, opening on the foam
　　　　Of perilous seas, in faery lands forlorn.

VIII

Forlorn! the very word is like a bell
    To toll me back from thee to my sole self!
Adieu! the fancy cannot cheat so well
    As she is fam'd to do, deceiving elf.
Adieu! adieu! thy plaintive anthem fades
      Past the near meadows, over the still stream,
        Up the hill-side; and now 'tis buried deep
        In the next valley-glades:
      Was it a vision, or a waking dream?
        Fled is that music:—Do I wake or sleep?

To a Skylark

Percy Bysshe Shelley

Hail to thee, blithe Spirit!
　　Bird thou never wert,
That from heaven, or near it,
　　Pourest thy full heart
In profuse strains of unpremeditated art.

Higher still and higher
　　From the earth thou springiest
Like a cloud of fire;
　　The blue deep thou wingest,
And singing still dost soar, and soaring ever singest.

In the golden lightning
　　Of the sunken sun,
O'er which clouds are bright'ning,
　　Thou dost float and run,
Like an unbodied joy whose race is just begun.

The pale purple even
　　Melts around thy flight;
Like a star of heaven
　　In the broad daylight
Thou art unseen, but yet I hear thy shrill delight—

Keen as are the arrows
　　Of that silver sphere

Whose intense lamp narrows
    In the white dawn clear,
Until we hardly see, we feel, that it is there.

All the earth and air
    With thy voice is loud,
As, when night is bare,
    From one lonely cloud
The moon rains out her beams, and heaven is
    overflowed.

What thou art we know not;
    What is most like thee?
From rainbow-clouds there flow not
    Drops so bright to see
As from thy presence showers a rain of melody:—

Like a poet hidden
    In the light of thought,
Singing hymns unbidden,
    Till the world is wrought
To sympathy with hopes and fears it heeded not:

Like a high-born maiden
    In a palace tower,
Soothing her love-laden
    Soul in secret hour
With music sweet as love, which overflows her
    bower:

Like a glow-worm golden
    In a dell of dew,

Scattering unbeholden
    Its aërial hue
Among the flowers and grass, which screen it from
    the view:

Like a rose embowered
    In its own green leaves,
By warm winds deflowered,
    Till the scent it gives
Makes faint with too much sweet these heavy-wingèd
    thieves:

Sound of vernal showers
    On the twinkling grass,
Rain-awakened flowers,—
    All that ever was,
Joyous, and clear, and fresh,—thy music doth surpass.

Teach us, sprite or bird,
    What sweet thoughts are thine:
I have never heard
    Praise of love or wine
That panted forth a flood of rapture so divine.

Chorus hymeneal
    Or triumphal chaunt,
Matched with thine, would be all
    But an empty vaunt—
A thing wherein we feel there is some hidden want.

What objects are the fountains
    Of thy happy strain?

What fields, or waves, or mountains?
　　　What shapes of sky or plain?
What love of thine own kind? what ignorance of pain?

　　With thy clear keen joyance
　　　　Languor cannot be:
　　Shadow of annoyance
　　　　Never came near thee:
Thou lovest, but ne'er knew love's sad satiety.

　　Waking or asleep,
　　　　Thou of death must deem
　　Things more true and deep
　　　　Than we mortals dream,
Or how could thy notes flow in such a crystal stream?

　　We look before and after,
　　　　And pine for what is not:
　　Our sincerest laughter
　　　　With some pain is fraught;
Our sweetest songs are those that tell of saddest
　　thought.

　　Yet if we could scorn
　　　　Hate, and pride, and fear;
　　If we were things born
　　　　Not to shed a tear,
I know not how thy joy we ever should come near.

　　Better than all measures
　　　　Of delightful sound,

Better than all treasures
        That in books are found,
Thy skill to poet were, thou scorner of the ground!

Teach me half the gladness
        That thy brain must know;
Such harmonious madness
        From my lips would flow
The world should listen then, as I am listening now.

The White Birds

William Butler Yeats

I would that we were, my beloved, white birds on the
    foam of the sea!
We tire of the flame of the meteor, before it can fade
    and flee;
And the flame of the blue star of twilight, hung low on
    the rim of the sky,
Has awaked in our hearts, my beloved, a sadness that
    may not die.

A weariness comes from those dreamers, dew dabbled,
    the lily and rose;
Ah, dream not of them, my beloved, the flame of the
    meteor that goes,
Or the flame of the blue star that lingers hung low in
    the fall of the dew:
For I would we were changed to white birds on the
    wandering foam: I and you!

I am haunted by numberless islands, and many a
    Danaan shore,
Where Time would surely forget us, and Sorrow come
    near us no more;
Soon far from the rose and the lily and fret of the flames
    would we be,
Were we only white birds, my beloved, buoyed out on
    the foam of the sea!

The Robin

John Greenleaf Whittier

My old Welsh neighbor over the way
　　Crept slowly out in the sun of spring,
Pushed from her ears the locks of gray,
　　And listened to hear the robin sing.

Her grandson, playing at marbles stopped,
　　And, cruel in sport as boys will be,
Tossed a stone at the bird, who hopped
　　From bough to bough in the apple-tree.

"Nay!" said the grandmother; "have you not heard,
　　My poor, bad boy! of the fiery pit,
And how, drop by drop, this merciful bird
　　Carries the water that quenches it?

"He brings cool dew in his little bill,
　　And lets it fall on the souls of sin:
You can see the mark on his red breast still
　　Of fires that scorch as he drops it in.

"My poor Bron rhuddyn! my breast-burned bird,
　　Singing so sweetly from limb to limb,
Very dear to the heart of Our Lord
　　Is he who pities the lost like Him!"

"Amen!" I said to the beautiful myth;
  "Sing, bird of God, in my heart as well:
Each good thought is a drop wherewith
  To cool and lessen the fires of hell.

"Prayers of love like rain-drops fall,
  Tears of pity are cooling dew,
And dear to the heart of Our Lord are all
  Who suffer like Him in the good they do!"

To a Waterfowl

William Cullen Bryant

Whither, midst falling dew,
While glow the heavens with the last steps of day
Far, through their rosy depths, dost thou pursue
    Thy solitary way?

Vainly the fowler's eye
Might mark thy distant flight to do thee wrong
As, darkly seen against the crimson sky,
    Thy figure floats along.

Seek'st thou the plashy brink
Of weedy lake, or marge of river wide,
Or where the rocking billows rise and sink
    On the chafed ocean side?

There is a Power whose care
Teaches thy way along that pathless coast—
The desert and illimitable air,—
    Lone wandering, but not lost.

All day thy wings have fanned,
At that far height, the cold, thin atmosphere,
Yet stoop not, weary, to the welcome land,
    Though the dark night is near.

And soon that toil shall end;
Soon shalt thou find a summer home, and rest,
And scream among thy fellows; reeds shall bend,
    Soon, o'er thy sheltered nest.

    Thou'rt gone, the abyss of heaven
Hath swallowed up thy form; yet, on my heart
Deeply has sunk the lesson thou hast given,
    And shall not soon depart.

    He who, from zone to zone,
Guides through the boundless sky thy certain flight,
In the long way that I must tread alone,
    Will lead my steps aright.

Sea

At Melville's Tomb

Hart Crane

Often beneath the wave, wide from this ledge
The dice of drowned men's bones he saw bequeath
An embassy. Their numbers as he watched,
Beat on the dusty shore and were obscured.

And wrecks passed without sound of bells,
The calyx of death's bounty giving back
A scattered chapter, livid hieroglyph,
The portent wound in corridors of shells.

Then in the circuit calm of one vast coil,
Its lashings charmed and malice reconciled,
Frosted eyes there were that lifted altars;
And silent answers crept across the stars.

Compass, quadrant and sextant contrive
No farther tides . . . High in the azure steeps
Monody shall not wake the mariner.
This fabulous shadow only the sea keeps.

By the Sea

Christina Rossetti

Why does the sea moan evermore?
    Shut out from heaven it makes its moan,
It frets against the boundary shore;
    All earth's full rivers cannot fill
    The sea, that drinking thirsteth still.

Sheer miracles of loveliness
    Lie hid in its unlooked-on bed:
Anemones, salt, passionless,
    Blow flower-like; just enough alive
    To blow and multiply and thrive.

Shells quaint with curve, or spot, or spike,
    Encrusted live things argus-eyed,
All fair alike, yet all unlike,
    Are born without a pang, and die
    Without a pang,—and so pass by.

A Sea-Side Walk

Elizabeth Barrett Browning

I

We walked beside the sea,
After a day which perished silently
Of its own glory—like the Princess weird
Who, combating the Genius, scorched and seared,
Uttered with burning breath, "Ho! victory!"
And sank adown, an heap of ashes pale;
    So runs the Arab tale.

II

The sky above us showed
An universal and unmoving cloud,
On which, the cliffs permitted us to see
Only the outline of their majesty,
As master-minds, when gazed at by the crowd!
And, shining with a gloom, the water grey
    Swang in its moon-taught way.

III

Nor moon nor stars were out.
They did not dare to tread so soon about,
Though trembling, in the footsteps of the sun.
The light was neither night's nor day's, but one
Which, life-like, had a beauty in its doubt;
And Silence's impassioned breathings round
    Seemed wandering into sound.

IV

O solemn-beating heart
Of nature! I have knowledge that thou art
Bound unto man's by cords he cannot sever—
And, what time they are slackened by him ever,
So to attest his own supernal part,
Still runneth thy vibration fast and strong,
    The slackened cord along.

V

    For though we never spoke
Of the grey water and the shaded rock,
Dark wave and stone, unconsciously, were fused
Into the plaintive speaking that we used,
Of absent friends and memories unforsook;
And, had we seen each other's face, we had
    Seen haply, each was sad.

A Hymn in Praise of Neptune

Thomas Campion

Of Neptune's empire let us sing,
At whose command the waves obey;
To whom the rivers tribute pay,
Down the high mountains sliding:
To whom the scaly nation yields
Homage for the crystal fields
     Wherein they dwell:
And every sea-god pays a gem
Yearly out of his wat'ry cell
To deck great Neptune's diadem.

The Tritons dancing in a ring
Before his palace gates do make
The water with their echoes quake,
Like the great thunder sounding:
The sea-nymphs chant their accents shrill,
And the sirens, taught to kill
     With their sweet voice,
Make ev'ry echoing rock reply
Unto their gentle murmuring noise
The praise of Neptune's empery.

The Kraken

Alfred, Lord Tennyson

Below the thunders of the upper deep,
Far, far beneath in the abysmal sea,
His ancient, dreamless, uninvaded sleep
The Kraken sleepeth: faintest sunlights flee
About his shadowy sides; above him swell
Huge sponges of millennial growth and height;
And far away into the sickly light,
From many a wondrous grot and secret cell
Unnumber'd and enormous polypi
Winnow with giant arms the slumbering green.
There hath he lain for ages, and will lie
Battening upon huge sea worms in his sleep,
Until the latter fire shall heat the deep;
Then once by man and angels to be seen,
In roaring he shall rise and on the surface die.

Sea Song

Katherine Mansfield

I will think no more of the sea!
Of the big green waves
And the hollowed shore,
Of the brown rock caves
No more, no more
Of the swell and the weed
And the bubbling foam.

Memory dwells in my far away home,
She has nothing to do with me.

She is old and bent
With a pack
On her back.
Her tears all spent,
Her voice, just a crack.
With an old thorn stick
She hobbles along,
And a crazy song
Now slow, now quick,
Wheeks in her throat.

And every day
While there's light on the shore
She searches for something;

Her withered claw
Tumbles the seaweed;
She pokes in each shell
Groping and mumbling
Until the night
Deepens and darkens,
And covers her quite,
And bids her be silent,
And bids her be still.

The ghostly feet
Of the whispery waves
Tiptoe beside her.
They follow, follow
To the rocky caves
In the white beach hollow . . .
She hugs her hands,
She sobs, she shrills,
And the echoes shriek
In the rocky hills.
She moans: "It is lost!
Let it be! Let it be!
I am old. I'm too cold.
I am frightened . . . the sea
Is too loud . . . it is lost,
It is gone . . ." Memory
Wails in my far away home.

What says the sea, little shell?

Stephen Crane

"What says the sea, little shell?
What says the sea?
Long has our brother been silent to us,
Kept his message for the ships,
Awkward ships, stupid ships."

"The sea bids you mourn, O Pines,
Sing low in the moonlight.
He sends tale of the land of doom,
Of place where endless falls
A rain of women's tears,
And men in grey robes—
Men in grey robes—
Chant the unknown pain."

"What says the sea, little shell?
What says the sea?
Long has our brother been silent to us,
Kept his message for the ships,
Puny ships, silly ships."

"The sea bids you teach, O Pines,
Sing low in the moonlight;
Teach the gold of patience,
Cry gospel of gentle hands,

Cry a brotherhood of hearts.
The sea bids you teach, O Pines."

"And where is the reward, little shell?
What says the sea?
Long has our brother been silent to us,
Kept his message for the ships,
Puny ships, silly ships."

"No word says the sea, O Pines,
No word says the sea.
Long will your brother be silent to you,
Keep his message for the ships,
O puny pines, silly pines."

The Ocean

Nathaniel Hawthorne

The Ocean has its silent caves,
Deep, quiet, and alone;
Though there be fury on the waves,
Beneath them there is none.
The awful spirits of the deep
Hold their communion there;
And there are those for whom we weep,
The young, the bright, the fair.

Calmly the wearied seamen rest
Beneath their own blue sea.
The ocean solitudes are blest,
For there is purity.
The earth has guilt, the earth has care,
Unquiet are its graves;
But peaceful sleep is ever there,
Beneath the dark blue waves.

Dover Beach

Matthew Arnold

The sea is calm tonight.
The tide is full, the moon lies fair
Upon the straits;—on the French coast the light
Gleams and is gone; the cliffs of England stand,
Glimmering and vast, out in the tranquil bay.
Come to the window, sweet is the night-air!
Only, from the long line of spray
Where the sea meets the moon-blanch'd land,
Listen! you hear the grating roar
Of pebbles which the waves draw back, and fling,
At their return, up the high strand,
Begin, and cease, and then again begin,
With tremulous cadence slow, and bring
The eternal note of sadness in.

Sophocles long ago
Heard it on the Ægean, and it brought
Into his mind the turbid ebb and flow
Of human misery; we
Find also in the sound a thought,
Hearing it by this distant northern sea.

The Sea of Faith
Was once, too, at the full, and round earth's shore
Lay like the folds of a bright girdle furled.

But now I only hear
Its melancholy, long, withdrawing roar,
Retreating, to the breath
Of the night-wind, down the vast edges drear
And naked shingles of the world.

Ah, love, let us be true
To one another! for the world, which seems
To lie before us like a land of dreams,
So various, so beautiful, so new,
Hath really neither joy, nor love, nor light,
Nor certitude, nor peace, nor help for pain;
And we are here as on a darkling plain
Swept with confused alarms of struggle and flight,
Where ignorant armies clash by night.

Sea-Change

Genevieve Taggard

You are no more, but sunken in a sea
Sheer into dream ten thousand leagues you fell;
And now you lie green-golden, while a bell
Swings with the tide, my heart. And all is well
Till I look down, and, wavering, the spell—
Your loveliness—returns. There in the sea,
Where you lie amber-pale and coral-cool,
You are most loved, most lost, most beautiful.

Land

Trees

Joyce Kilmer

I think that I shall never see
A poem lovely as a tree.

A tree whose hungry mouth is prest
Against the earth's sweet flowing breast;

A tree that looks at God all day,
And lifts her leafy arms to pray;

A tree that may in Summer wear
A nest of robins in her hair;

Upon whose bosom snow has lain;
Who intimately lives with rain.

Poems are made by fools like me,
But only God can make a tree.

Loveliest of trees, the cherry now

A. E. Housman

Loveliest of trees, the cherry now
Is hung with bloom along the bough,
And stands about the woodland ride
Wearing white for Eastertide.

Now, of my threescore years and ten,
Twenty will not come again,
And take from seventy springs a score,
It only leaves me fifty more.

And since to look at things in bloom
Fifty springs are little room,
About the woodlands I will go
To see the cherry hung with snow.

Overhead the Tree-Tops Meet

Robert Browning

Overhead the tree-tops meet,
Flowers and grass spring 'neath one's feet;
There was nought above me, nought below,
My childhood had not learned to know:
For what are the voices of birds
—Ay, and of beasts,—but words, our words,
Only so much more sweet?
The knowledge of that with my life begun!
But I had so near made out the sun,
And counted your stars, the seven and one,
Like the fingers of my hand:
Nay, I could all but understand
Wherefore through heaven the white moon ranges;
And just when out of her soft fifty changes
No unfamiliar face might overlook me—
Suddenly God took me!

The Eagle Trees

Sarah Orne Jewett

Great pines that watch the river go
Down to the sea all night, all day,
Firm-rooted near its ebb and flow,
Bowing their heads to winds at play,
Strong-limbed and proud, they silent stand,
And watch the mountains far away,
And watch the miles of farming land,
And hear the church bells tolling slow.

They see the men in distant fields
Follow the furrows of the plough;
They count the loads the harvest yields,
And fight the storms with every bough,
Beating the wild winds back again.
The April sunshine cheers them now;
They eager drink the warm spring rain,
Nor dread the spear the lightning wields.

High in the branches clings the nest
The great birds build from year to year;
And though they fly from east to west,
Some instinct keeps this eyrie dear
To their fierce hearts; and now their eyes
Glare down at me with rage and fear;
They stare at me with wild surprise,
Where high in air they strong-winged rest.

Companionship of birds and trees!
The years have proved your friendship strong
You share each other's memories,
The river's secret and its song,
And legends of the country-side:
The eagles take their journeys long,
The great trees wait in noble pride
For messages from hills and seas.

I hear a story that you tell
In idleness of summer days:
A singer that the world knows well
To you again in boyhood strays;
Within the stillness of your shade
He rests where flickering sunlight plays,
And sees the nests the eagles made,
And wonders at the distant bell.

His keen eyes watch the forest growth,
The rabbits' fear, the thrushes' flight;
He loiters gladly, nothing loath
To be alone at fall of night.
The woodland things around him taught
Their secrets in the evening light,
Whispering some wisdom to his thought
Known to the pines and eagles both.

Was it the birds who early told
The dreaming boy that he would win
A poet's crown instead of gold?
That he would fight a nation's sin?—
On eagle wings of song would gain

A place that few might enter in,
And keep his life without a stain
Through many years, yet not grow old?

And he shall be what few men are,
Said all the pine-trees, whispering low;
His thought shall find an unseen star;
He shall our treasured legends know;
His words will give the way-worn rest
Like this cool shade our branches throw;
He, lifted like our loftiest crest,
Shall watch his country near and far.

The Dandelion

Vachel Lindsay

O dandelion, rich and haughty,
King of village flowers!
Each day is coronation time,
You have no humble hours.
I like to see you bring a troop
To beat the blue-grass spears,
To scorn the lawn-mower that would be
Like fate's triumphant shears,
Your yellow heads are cut away,
It seems your reign is o'er.
By noon you raise a sea of stars
More golden than before.

To the Violet

John Clare

Sweet tiny flower of darkly hue,
    Lone dweller in the pathless shade;
How much I love thy pensive blue
    Of innocence so well display'd!

What time the watery skies are full
    Of streaming dappled clouds so pale,
And sideling rocks, more white than wool,
    Portending snowy sleet, or hail;

I 'gin to seek thy charming flower
    Along each hedge-row's mossy seat,
Where, dithering many a cold bleak hour,
    I've hugg'd myself in thy retreat.

What makes me cherish such fond taste,
    What makes such raptures spring for thee,
Is, that thou lov'st the dreary waste
    Which is so well belov'd by me.

For solitude should be my choice
    Could I this labouring life resign,
To see the little birds rejoice,
    And thy sweet flowers in clusters shine.

I'd choose a cave beside some rock,
    Clos'd in all round with ash and thorn,
That near my door thy tribe might flock
    To shed their sweets in early morn.

But, ah! that way would never prove
    Means to sustain impending life;
I must forego those scenes I love,
    And still beat on with needy strife.

Sweet flower! we must reverse the plan,
    Nor cherish such romantic views;
I'll strive to seek thee when I can,
    Through noontide heat or evening dews.

To spring return, with all thy train
    Of flowrets cloth'd in varied hue,
I long to see that morn again
    Which brings to light the violet blue.

The Lamb

William Blake

Little Lamb, who made thee?
Does thou know who made thee,
Gave thee life, and bade thee feed.
By the stream and o'er the mead;
Gave thee clothing of delight,
Softest clothing woolly bright;
Gave thee such a tender voice.
Making all the vales rejoice?
    Little Lamb who made thee?
    Does thou know who made thee?

Little Lamb I'll tell thee;
Little Lamb I'll tell thee:
He is called by thy name,
For he calls himself a Lamb.
He is meek, and He is mild,
He became a little child
I a child, and thou a lamb,
We are callèd by His name,
    Little Lamb God bless thee!
    Little Lamb God bless thee!

A Noiseless, Patient Spider

Walt Whitman

A noiseless patient spider,
I mark'd where on a little promontory it stood isolated,
Mark'd how to explore the vacant vast surrounding,
It launch'd forth filament, filament, filament, out of
    itself,
Ever unreeling them, ever tirelessly speeding them.

And you O my soul where you stand,
Surrounded, detached, in measureless oceans of space,
Ceaselessly musing, venturing, throwing, seeking the
    spheres to connect them,
Till the bridge you will need be form'd, till the ductile
    anchor hold,
Till the gossamer thread you fling catch somewhere,
    O my soul.

The Andante of Snakes

Arthur Symons

They weave a slow andante as in sleep,
Scaled yellow, swampy black, plague-spotted white;
With blue and lidless eyes at watch they keep
A treachery of silence; infinite

Ancestral angers brood in these dull eyes
Where the long-lineaged venom of the snake
Meditates evil; woven intricacies
Of Oriental arabesque awake,

Unfold, expand, contract, and raise and sway
Swoln heart-shaped heads, flattened as by a heel,
Erect to suck the sunlight from the day,
And stealthily and gradually reveal

Dim cabalistic signs of spots and rings
Among their folds of faded tapestry;
Then these fat, foul, unbreathing, moving things
Droop back to stagnant immobility.

To a Mouse

On Turning Her Up in Her Nest
with the Plough

Robert Burns

Wee, sleekit, cow'rin', tim'rous beastie,
O what a panic's in thy breastie!
Thou need na start awa sae hasty,
  Wi' bickering brattle!
I wad be laith to rin an' chase thee
  Wi' murd'ring *pattle!*

 I'm truly sorry man's dominion
Has broken Nature's social union,
An' justifies that ill opinion
  Which makes thee startle
At me, thy poor earth-born companion,
  An' *fellow-mortal!*

 I doubt na, whyles, but thou may thieve;
What then? poor beastie, thou maun live!
A *daimen-icker* in a *thrave*
  'S a sma' request:
I'll get a blessin' wi' the lave,
  And never miss't!

 Thy wee bit *housie*, too, in ruin!
Its silly wa's the win's are strewin':

An' naething, now, to big a new ane,
      O' foggage green!
An' bleak December's winds ensuin'
        Baith snell an' keen!

      Thou saw the fields laid bare and waste
An' weary winter comin' fast,
An' cozie here, beneath the blast,
      Thou thought to dwell,
Till, crash! the cruel *coulter* past
      Out thro' thy cell.

      That wee bit heap o' leaves an' stubble
Has cost thee mony a weary nibble!
Now thou's turned out, for a' thy trouble,
      But house or hald,
To thole the winter's sleety dribble
      An' cranreuch cauld!

      But, Mousie, thou art no thy lane
In proving *foresight* may be vain:
The best laid schemes o' *mice* an' men
      Gang aft agley,
An' lea'e us nought but grief an' pain,
      For promised joy.

      Still thou art blest, compared wi' *me!*
The *present* only toucheth thee:
But, Och! I backward cast my e'e
      On prospects drear:
An' forward, tho' I canna *see,*
      I *guess* an' *fear!*

Nature's Questioning

Thomas Hardy

When I look forth at dawning, pool,
    Field, flock, and lonely tree,
    All seem to look at me
Like chastened children sitting silent in a school;

Their faces dulled, constrained, and worn,
    As though the master's ways
    Through the long teaching days
Their first terrestrial zest had chilled and overborne.

Upon them stirs, in lippings mere
    (As if once clear in call,
    But now scarce breathed at all)—
"We wonder, ever wonder, why we find us here!

"Has some Vast Imbecility,
    Mighty to build and blend,
    But impotent to tend,
Framed us in jest, and left us now to hazardry?

"Or come we of an Automaton
    Unconscious of our pains?. . .
    Or are we live remains
Of Godhead dying downwards, brain and eye now gone?

"Or is it that some high Plan betides,
    As yet not understood,
    Of Evil stormed by Good,
We the Forlorn Hope over which Achievement strides?"

Thus things around. No answerer I. . . .
    Meanwhile the winds, and rains,
    And Earth's old glooms and pains
Are still the same, and gladdest Life Death neighbors nigh.

There will come soft rains

(War Time)

Sara Teasdale

There will come soft rains and the smell of the ground,
And swallows circling with their shimmering sound;

And frogs in the pools singing at night,
And wild plum-trees in tremulous white;

Robins will wear their feathery fire
Whistling their whims on a low fence-wire;

And not one will know of the war, not one
Will care at last when it is done.

Not one would mind, neither bird nor tree
If mankind perished utterly;

And Spring herself, when she woke at dawn,
Would scarcely know that we were gone.

Signature Select Classics

Elegantly Designed Booklets of Poetry and Prose

This book is part of Sterling Publishing's Signature Select Classics chapbook series. Each booklet features distinguished poetry and prose by the world's greatest poets and writers in an elegantly designed and printed chapbook binding. These books are essential reading for lovers of classic literature and collectible editions in their own right. They make perfect keepsakes to own and to share with others.